LECTURE

ON THE

DUTIES AND RELATIONS

OF

PARENTS, TEACHERS AND PUPILS,

AS

CONNECTED WITH EDUCATION.

BY CHARLES DAVIES,

DELIVERED AT THE FIRST SESSION OF THE TEACHERS' INSTITUTE,
HELD UNDER THE DIRECTION OF THE BOARD OF EDUCATION,
AT THE NORMAL SCHOOL AT YPSILANTI, MICHIGAN,
1852.

DETROIT:
FREE PRESS BOOK AND JOB OFFICE PRINT.

1852.

PUBLISHED BY DIRECTION

OF

THE BOARD OF EDUCATION.

LECTURE.

The great problem of the present age is the education of the young.

The diffusion of knowledge among men—the analysis of the rights of man, as an intelligent, social and accountable being—a careful examination of the laws of civil society and of the social relations, have awakened humanity from the slumber of ages, and it now appears on the stage of human action, armed with the justice of its own claims and bold in the assertion of its divine origin.

Before these mighty powers of the 19th century thrones have crumbled—old institutions have disappeared, and now the dawn of a brighter day excites the hopes and gladdens the heart of philanthropy. Although the struggle may be long, and the progress of truth, justice and intelligence occasionally impeded, they must and will ultimately triumph.

It is ordained of Providence that great changes in the condition of the world be gradual, and that they be brought about by appropriate means. Such means appear to be in a course of rapid development.

The Press scatters its burning sheets throughout the entire region of civilization. Commerce spreads her sails on every ocean, and in every commercial metropolis the flags of all nations float together in the same breeze. The earth has been girded with iron bands, over which the chariots of trade pass with dizzying velocity. Steam has also added its gigantic power, and sets space and the elements at defiance. It sweeps the ocean with a giant's stride, and has established new connections and sympathies in the family of nations. So close are those connections, and so intimate are those sympathies, that not a gun is fired on the banks of the Danube whose reverberation is not heard along our whole Atlantic coast and through the entire valley of the Mississippi.

In this age of rapid development and impetuous discovery, time has been annihilated. The sun himself has been outstripped in his daily circuit, by thought, which travels with its own wonted rapidity along wires constructed by the hand of man. The heavens have also been explored by new and powerful instruments—new planets have been added to our system, and new systems have also been discovered lying far in the infinitude of space.

The present generation has been permitted to witness, and in some degree to participate in the development of these great events—events which are yet to exert an unmeasured influence on the family of man.

Apart from that general condition of the world which distinguishes the age in which we live from any that has been recorded in the volume of history, is there anything peculiar in the condition of our own country which calls for special efforts in the training and education of the young?

From a moral summit higher than the Andes, we have unfurled the banner of universal freedom and beckoned to the oppressed of the earth to come here and repose under its ample folds. The protection of that banner is committed to the virtue, the intelligence and the patriotism of this people. From the rocky shores and ice-bound coast of Nova Scotia to the sunny climes of the Gulf of Mexico—from the broad Atlantic to the great inland seas—and from the Father of Waters to the distant shores of California and Oregon, one government and one flag give repose and happiness to a people speaking a common language—the government is one of their own choice—the flag, the emblem of freedom, and the language that of Shakspeare and Milton—our own loved English.

Such is the inheritance of the present generation—how great its blessings—how great, also, its responsibilities. How are these institutions which promise so much for posterity—institutions founded by the virtue and cemented by the blood of our fathers—to be preserved—enlarged—made permanent? They are founded on the intelligence and virtue of the people, and hence can only be maintained by a system of public instruction reaching all who share in the government—holding up to the mind the light of intelligence, and to the heart the standard of duty. This, then, brings us to the question of education—and what is it?

Education is that system of training which develops in their right direction and in their proper proportions, our physical, intellectual and moral natures.

By the term physical, we mean all that relates to the body—to its health, form and proper development. In the term intellectual, we include all the faculties of the mind which enable us to acquire ideas—to remember them—to compare them with each other, and to develop new ones from the relations existing between those already known. In this class are the faculties of apprehension, memory, judgment, and the reasoning powers. By the moral nature, we mean the whole class of the affections—the emotions of joy and sorrow—of pleasure and pain—of love and hatred—of stoical indifference and tender sympathy—and of faith, which springs from the heart and guides the life.

With these three elements of our common nature, the teacher has to deal continually. He has to watch over the physical—to guard the health—to see that the body is kept constantly in the right position—that all its parts are perfectly developed—that exercise is duly mixed with intellectual labor, and that the body be not over-tasked.

Over the mind he must be ever watchful. It is a tender plant, and he must nurture it with maternal care.

The moral nature of his pupils will be, with the teacher, a subject of earnest and constant solicitude. Their young affections will need his warmest sympathies for their growth and development.

With the general impressions resulting from this simple analysis, let us suppose a teacher to enter the school-room for the first time. What is the first step to be taken? What are the first things to be done? To establish his authority over his school—to ensure the obedience of his scholars—to win their confidence—to gain their respect, and to call into exercise their warmest affections. And how are these results to be attained?

1st. By a system of inflexible justice—by the establishment of general rules applicable equally to all—and to which all are equally required to yield the same obedience. All the scholars of a school stand, in regard to their teacher, on the same level. Each has an equal claim to his instructions—his encouraging words—his forbearance—and, also, to the steadiness and firmness of his discipline. To them all, he should feel himself equally allied. He is the officer appointed by the public authority to watch over and rear up the children of the republic. He holds an official station—is charged with responsible duties, and the individual should be merged in the public officer. He should ever hold the scales of justice with a bandage over his eyes. He should be certain that individual preferences exert no influence; and yet, the feeling should ever be present both in his mind and heart, that justice to the young must always be tempered with kindness.

2d. The teacher must always be consistent with himself. Uniformity, in system and conduct, is indispensable to the exercise of control and influence over others. A dignified, calm and courteous manner, with words appropriately and kindly spoken, will awaken a response in the young heart, of respect, love and obedience. Familiarity, which sinks the teacher in the companion, will render necessary at a subsequent period, the exercise of a sterner authority—and this will break that uniformity of manner and conduct which is one of the main anchors of control over the minds of the young. That manner, which, at the same time, cultivates the affections and ensures the respect of the pupils—which establishes a current of warm sympathy and a cheerful and ready obedience founded on love and a principle of duty, should be the aim and study of every teacher.

It is a great mistake, however, to suppose that it is desirable to appeal to the affections only, as a means of government. Obedience is a proper submission to rightful authority. Such submission should be taught and insisted on, both in the family and in the school room, and the teacher will fail in one of his most important duties, if he do not inculcate the principle, that the relations of himself and pupils demand the exercise of a rightful authority on his part, and a cheerful obedience on theirs, as a duty equally obligatory on both.

To preserve that consistency with oneself, necessary to the establishment and maintenance of authority, with the least possible discipline, requires watchfulness and self-control. Great care must be observed that every order given to a pupil, be punctually and cheerfully obeyed. If James receives a command which is distasteful to him, in a tone leaving any doubt on his mind in regard to the unalterable purpose of his teacher, he will pause and hesitate, and finally ask if certain things more pressing ought not to have precedence? At first, these remonstrances should be answered by the firm and kind reply, James, did you not understand me? or, James, it is a rule of this school that every order be promptly and cheerfully obeyed, without objection or delay. If James still persists, he must be punished until he will go silently and immediately to the performance of the duty assigned him. Establish the principle, at any cost of needful discipline, that every order which you give must be obeyed without murmur and without objection. Be careful, then, never to give an order either trifling or unjust in its nature, or beyond the scope of your legitimate authority. This done, see that all your orders are promptly and silently obeyed. You will thus acquire the entire and perfect control of your school.

Passion and violence will ever injure the authority of a teacher. They discover a weakness and a want of self-control which the child is quick to discern, and they arouse in his own breast a feeling of opposition and a sense of injury. There is a firm and gentle tone, and a calm and dignified manner, which impel to obedience, and these will often prevail when correction, even with the rod, fails of its effect.

Too much talking about the necessity of obedience, and especially threatening punishment, will soon loose their effect on the mind of the pupil, and will ever weaken the authority of a teacher. Perhaps there is no one cause which operates so certainly to produce this result as a too great willingness on the part of a teacher to explain his motives—and a too earnest desire to be rightly understood by those whom he may have to correct—and a too sensitive fear lest his scholars should feel that he has been unjust or even unnecessarily severe. All this, teachers, will tend to subvert the order of your schools—to place your pupils in the attitude of critics and judges, and yourselves in the humiliating position of accounting to them for your conduct. Silence exerts a powerful influence over the minds of the young, and is a great aid and support of authority. Be careful, therefore, never, by raising the curtain, to disclose to your pupils what you think and feel in regard to yourself. Hold free and open intercourse with them on all matters of instruction—lay open to them every subject of knowledge to which you ask their attention—fathom their hearts and direct their sympathies in the channels best calculated to expand and develop them—but do nothing, either by word or act, which shall justify them in analyzing your conduct, scanning your motives or placing themselves in the judgment seat to pronounce upon your doings. Above all things, never admit into your hearts, for a single moment, the idea that you and your pupils stand in the position of antagonism. Never make yourselves a party in opposition to them. It is your duty to govern and teach—theirs to obey and learn. You must put on patience as a garment and wear it always.

We come next, teachers, to the methods of imparting instruction.

It is a trite remark, and yet must ever be borne in mind, that it is the primary object of education so to train the mind and form the moral character, that when the pupil leaves the Academy or College Hall, he may go forth prepared to discharge those duties, and fulfil those destinies, which an all-wise Providence has appointed to us here. Hence, teachers, it should be your object to train the mind to self-action—to strengthen and develop all its faculties—to accustom it, even in its very first efforts, to original combinations—and to give it a foundation and centering of its own. Masses of knowledge, like masses of matter, are capable of being separated into very minute portions or elements. These should be presented to the mind separately, and in their proper order. *Teach one thing at a time—teach that thing thoroughly—and as far as possible, teach all its connections with other things!*

There is as much skill necessary to teach a child the alphabet and the first combination of sounds, as is required to instruct him in the higher branches of Geometry. Indeed, when the mind is weak and feeble—unaccustomed to action, credulous, and easily led, more care is necessary in giving it a proper direction than is required, afterwards, to keep it in the right path.

In all your teachings, be careful to be *distinct* and *definite.* Be sure that every question which you put has a distinct and appropriate answer—and then see that that answer is given, and accept of no other. When you put a question, however unimportant, give the pupil full time to reflect upon it before he answers—and do not allow him to answer at a venture, or before he has fully considered the nature and scope of the question.

You would not, after having put in motion a delicate and complicated piece of machinery, suddenly to arrest that motion. Were you to do so, you would derange its action and perhaps break or destroy some of its essential parts. Would you, then, after exciting the mental energies to action—after waking up, as it were, the young mind, suddenly to arrest it in its trains of thought, at the moment it was putting forth its powers? The young are naturally distrustful of themselves, and the greatest care should be taken not to thwart or discourage them in their first mental efforts.

When you put a question to a pupil, he must first apprehend the nature of that question; he must then consider the nature of the answer, after which he must select from his own limited vocabulary the best words in which to express that answer. Thus, you see, there are several mental operations before he is ready to respond. You cannot be too particular in the matter of not interfering, by a series of rapid questions, with the mental operations of your pupils. Indeed, I may say, that to abstain from doing so, lies at the foundation of all good teaching. Let every question which you put elicit one distinct idea or thought, and see that the answer brings out that thought, fully and distinctly. But let it come out in its own way—let the mind of the pupil conceive and frame the answer.

If you wish to guide or direct the mind into a particular channel, do it by a series of gentle and dependent inductions. Follow the analogy of nature. See how the mother teaches the child to walk. She first partially supports it, until it can stand alone, then she places one foot before the other, until nature, co-operating with her efforts, brings about the desired result. Similarly with our intellectual efforts. The eye of the teacher must be quick to discern the strength of mind and aptness of his scholar. He must not tax his mind too heavily—he must not leave it to itself; but by tasks adapted to its capacity, must tempt it from effort to effort, as the young eagle is taught to fly from branch to branch, before it is able to soar aloft and gaze upon the sun.

After the mind of the pupil has been impressed with a sufficient number of distinct elementary ideas, the next step in his intellectual development is to combine those ideas: that is, to put them together in such a manner as to deduce new ones, having a legitimate and logical connection with those already known.

For example, after having learned the sounds of the letters of the alphabet, the child must next be taught to combine those sounds, forming words; and by combining these words in a certain order we form a rich and fruitful language, which becomes the vehicle of our thoughts and feelings. Thus, by the simple process of combination, wonderful results are obtained. Twenty-six simple characters, each representing one or more distinct sounds or modulations of the human voice, are put together in sets, called words; and these words may be so arranged as to express every thought of the mind and every feeling of the heart. I give this merely as an illustration of the results which may be deduced by the combination of simple elements.

The habit of classification and association will both improve the memory and strengthen the power of analysis. It sharpens and brightens the mind—gives it a clear and penetrating power and cultivates the faculties of comparison and judgment. The reasoning faculty, which evolves new truths from the relations that exist between known premises, cannot be fully developed without the aid of these preliminary steps. This is the great governing faculty of the mind. It is to the intellect what mathematics is to general science.

In all your teachings, you should keep the separate faculties of the mind constantly in view. You will find them to exist in different intensity in the several pupils of the same school. With some, it will be difficult to make the first step. You will often have to labor much to impress a single distinct idea—

to give a single impression that shall leave its trace upon the mind. Others will apprehend with readiness, but remember with difficulty—while others, still differently constituted, will not only apprehend quickly but remember with surprising tenacity, and yet be unable either to compare or combine their ideas. Such will be regarded as matter-of-fact men. They possess no original powers—will travel the old and known road—will invent nothing and add little to the common stock of human knowledge.

Others, by a too rapid association, will condine and compare with too much facility. Their minds fly from object to object with such celerity of motion and such indistinctness of mental vision, that nothing is clearly understood. They have not the patience to think deeply and accurately. Their minds, long indulged in the vagrant habit of touching things only on the surface, become impatient of restraint and averse to labor. They see, indeed, but it is "through a glass darkly;" and their perceptions, are like the visions of a dream, associated in wild and fanciful combinations.

In the cultivation and development of these intellectual faculties, it should be your object, teachers, to bring them forward in their just proportions. Some, it is true, may be more important than others, but each and all are necessary to form a perfect whole, as each color of the rainbow is required to make up the perfect light of day. They are, indeed, like the finished columns of a temple; they at once support and adorn the mental edifice.

But, teachers, while you are especially anxious to develop those powers which give to the mind its strength and vigor, you must not neglect the cultivation of the secondary faculties which constitute its grace and ornament.

The love of the beautiful, either in nature or art, is one of those sympathies implanted in the soul for wise and beneficent purposes, and should be carefully and assiduously cultivated. In your daily readings, in the school-room, you will have many opportunities of awakening in the minds of your pupils a taste for the beauties of fine writing. You may, with great advantage, point out to them the striking passages of their lessons—dwell on the poetic associations which excited the imaginations of their authors, and thus awaken in their minds a warmer and more genial spirit than is elicited by efforts merely intellectual.

You should also ever be ready to open the minds of your pupils to a nice perception of the beauties of nature.

Whoever walked forth at "early dawn or dewy eve" without feeling the wisdom and beneficence of that Being who clothes the fields in verdure and has filled the heavens with the light of his countenance? Who ever gazed on the mountain, or lifted his eyes to the starry heavens without a deep impression of the majesty of God? Who ever surveyed the verdant meadow—with its flocks cropping the grass—or looked upon the placid lake, or the smiling fields waving with the ripened harvest, without a grateful emotion to the kind Providence who has spread so much beauty around us?

Opportunities may occur, in the discharge of your duties as teachers, to plant in the virgin soil of the young mind the seeds of such delightful impressions. Sow them, broad-cast, whenever and wherever you can. Some may fall among thorns—some by the way-side—

but much will fall upon good soil and bring forth fruit abundantly.

But, teachers, your responsibilities by no means terminate in the physical and intellectual instruction which you may impart. You are, also, the moral teachers of youth. All their affections are committed to your care. If you do not preside at the birth, you do at the baptism of their moral nature — and *that* is the basis of all subsequent religious impression and belief. The affections are to the intellect what the forge is to the metal—they soften and shape it, and give to it those attractive forms which augment its power and heighten its beauty.

The principle which lies at the foundation of this class of feelings, is an *obedient faith*—by which I mean that *confidence* in another which impels to obedience in his authority alone. It is this feeling of faith which prompts the obedient child to feel that the commands of his parents are right, and that he ought to obey them because of the authority from which they emanate. It is this feeling which imparts to the good boy at school that confiding trust in his teacher which will not permit him to question his authority, or scan his motives —but which produces a prompt and ready obedience. In all your teaching, strive to cultivate this feeling. The spirit which is imbued with it, will conduct its possessor along the road of obedience and order—will make him orderly at school—obedient at home—a citizen observing the laws—and on to such a spirit is easily engrafted that religious faith which reaches beyond the transitory things of this life and lays hold on the rich promises of that which is to come.

There is nothing which you should labor more earnestly to discourage and repress than a captious spirit of doubting. Hold no terms with the disposition to reject everything not proved by rigorous demonstration. It is, I know, supposed by some, to be a certain indication of genius to believe nothing. Hence, some have gone so far as to doubt even of their own existence. Such can have no well founded confidence in God or man. They must pass through life in a state of alienation from their fellow beings—denying the existence of virtue as an active principle—exploring every road which opens before them because they will not believe the guide boards; and finally, sinking down into the grave under the dark cloud of a settled scepticism.

In order to give full effect to your teachings, and especially to inspire your pupils with that implicit confidence which we have denominated faith—you must be ever on your guard to be perfectly truthful in all your intercourse with them. I do not mean by this caution to imply that you would willingly deceive them either by word or deed. That you may not do this, you must never fail to carry out, at all times, and under all circumstances, everything which you have given them to understand that you would do. If you tell John that you will punish him if he whispers—and he then whispers, you must do as you said, at all hazards, however sorry he may be for having offended, or however painful it may be to your feelings. If you do not, he will distrust you, and that delightful principle, an obedient faith, will have received an injury.

We are not, in general, sufficiently impressed with the influence which slight causes often exert over the minds of the young. A successful trick, or a skillful manœuvre—perhaps partially commended because evincing tact or smartness, often changes forever its destinies. At the sources of streams, little pebbles will change their entire direction and determine into what sea or ocean their waters shall finally flow.

Be careful, therefore, in dealing with the moral nature of your pupils to give the first development in the right direction. If the body is wounded, the wound may be healed, but a scar will remain, and the part never again will be perfect as before. Think you that if an injury be inflicted on that more delicate part of our being, our moral nature, that will heal and leave no trace behind? None may be seen—the effects even may not be decerned by a human eye. But will not that eye which sees our mental and moral natures as plainly as our eyes can decern the physical, clearly perceive all that weakens the one or impairs the other? Therefore, ever bear in mind that you are dealing with beings fearfully and wonderfully made; and that the lessons which you teach and the influences you exert, may not only form their characters here, but decide those more important destinies which lie beyond the grave.

We find, in children, at a very early age, the indications of those principles of good and evil which constitute the warring elements of our moral nature. Passion—self-indulgence—impatience of restraint—burst forth even within the walls of the nursery; but affection—docility—endurance, are also there. That struggle between good and evil, which is recorded in heaven, begins with the dawn of life and terminates only with the last gasp of decaying nature.

It has been a great problem with educators to discover which of these principles is most to be dealt with—whether the good is to be mainly cultivated, and in its growth and development to overcome and crowd out the evil—or, whether the evil principle is first to be eradicated in order to prepare the soil for the seeds of virtue. Experience and a close analysis of the mind and affections would seem to indicate, that we are mainly to address ourselves to that which bears the good fruit, and that the tares, which cannot be plucked up without destroying the wheat also, must be left until the final harvest.

Let us, therefore, cultivate and strengthen

the good. If the child is passionate, do not increase the evil by severe punishment, administered under a like spirit, thereby adding the element of hatred; but labor, rather, to cultivate the spirit of gentleness and self-control. If he is self-indulgent, do not deprive him of all amusement and gratification. If he is perverse and obstinate, let the soft influences of gentleness tame and subdue his stubborn spirit. Thus, ever apply the antidotes than aggravate the disease.

There is one class of pupils which will fall under your care, (for they are found more or less in every school,) for whom I would bespeak, especially, your indulgence and kindness. I refer to those who seem to be the *orphans* rather than the *favorites* of Providence—those, who in mental and moral endowment are below the level of their companions. They will come to you from homes where they may have been regarded as inferior members of the household. Discouragement and despair will be written on their faces, and the inspirations of hope will have ceased to warm their young bosoms. In such, a deep sense of inferiority weighs down the buoyancy of youth, and they are ready to sink into despondency or to envelop themselves in the gloom of a sullen despair. To such, be ever patient, kind and gentle. Let no jest, or taunt, or scornful look, or disparaging comparison, bruise the broken reed and sink lower the young spirit made prematurely old by a painful sense of its own inferiority. Let your kindness, rather, fall upon such spirits with the same gentleness as do the dews of heaven upon the opening flowers, and they may bring forth the beauty of full fruition.

You, who have embraced the vocation of teachers and assumed the responsible duties of giving instruction to the young, occupy places of more commanding importance than those who sit in the halls of legislation or preside in our courts of justice. To you, is emphatically committed the formation of the intellectual, and to a certain extent, the moral character of this people. You not only hold in your hands the keys of knowledge, but you have the power to give such a direction to the young minds, committed to your care, as shall inspire them with a love of virtue, or turn them into the dark alleys of ignorance and vice.

Your calling, however honorable as it is, is beset on every side with embarrassment and difficulty—and this, mainly, because the public do not understand the importance and dignity of your vocation.

The lawyer, who is to adjust the rights of property, must be regularly educated at the school, the academy and the college. This even will not suffice, and he is further trained in the office and the law school. The clergyman, also, must be thoroughly educated. He must pass through all the schools—study profoundly, and receive much special preparation before he is deemed qualified to discharge the high trusts he is to assume. The physician, who is to heal the body, is not allowed to practice his profession till he has waded through volumes of profound science—heard medical lectures—attended medical schools and given evidence of high attainments.

Those, even, who are to copy physical nature are more cared for than they who are to develop the mental and moral. The sculptor is not deemed competent to mould the human form until he has made a pilgrimage to the Vatican and studied there the sublime forms which were shaped by the genius of antiquity. The painter feels that he cannot give full expression to the human face unless he visits the galleries of Italy and catches inspiration from the immortal canvass of Raphael. But how is it with the teacher? Where are the institutions for his instruction and education? Until recently, he has been picked up by the wayside. A lawyer without briefs—a clergyman who cannot preach—a merchant who has failed, or a mechanic without work, have been thought to answer well enough for the school-room, and the compensation has been adjusted according to the same scale as for work done with the hands. This can no longer be so. The ample provisions made by your own State for the education of teachers, shows that, though young in years, she is yet old in wisdom.

The expectations, also, in regard to what teachers can accomplish, are often very erroneous. Many suppose that you can, at once, in a single term, mould the stubborn will of an ungoverned boy to cheerful obedience—and this, by the gentle process of moral suasion. It is confidently hoped by the anxious parent, that the noisy and resisting child at home, will become the gentle and docile scholar of the school. It is not even supposed that positive resistence to parental authority is any indication of the want of a right spirit towards a teacher. You will, therefore, in many cases, not receive from the parent that support in the maintenance of your authority which even-handed justice demands. You will often see the child upheld when he is wrong and your authority set at nought, when the best interests of the child require that it should be supported. You will see a short-sighted parental attachment prevailing over an enlarged view of the real interests of the scholar. You will see the seeds of insubordination scattered in the young mind even by the parental hand—there to vegetate—to bring forth in youth disobedience and disorder, and in after life, contempt of all law, human and divine.

Amid all these causes of discouragement and mortification, it is expected that the teacher will be perfectly tranquil and always right. In your case, no allowances will be made for the infirmities of human nature. No excuses will be offered up on the shrine of maternal love for your mistakes or misdeeds. You will be held to a rigid accountability, and sometimes before the uncertain tribunal of public opinion.

Among those who are without experience in the vocations to which you have dedicated yourselves, a most mistaken opinion prevails both in regard to the difficulties and labor of teaching. It is supposed, that to talk six hours a day is no great affair, and that such sciences ought not to be paid more highly than the same amount of labor done with the hands. You who have had the care of schools, know full well, how great is the error of such opinions. I need not to describe to you how soon the constant care of a large school makes its impression both on the mind and body. You have all, doubtless, observed how soon the school-room changes the ruddy complexion and gives to the tranquil and happy face an expression of anxiety and care.

It is an old adage, that constant dropping wears a stone. It is equally true that a constant effort of the mind and a continued excitement of the feelings will soon make their impressions on the strongest intellect and the most robust body.

The constant exhaustion of the body and mind which is produced by teaching is not restored by that relaxation and variety of pursuit which are found in the other professions. The teacher takes his place in the school-room by the road-side—and there day in and day out, toils away his life in subduing the refractory, and in planting in the young mind the seeds of knowledge.

The eyes of the world are, in a measure, withdrawn from him. No anxious multitude applauds him—no senate chamber resounds with his eloquence—no public press teams with his praises, and no sympathy of friends cheers him in his daily labors. Each day brings with it the same round of duties, and each evening the same fatigue and exhaustion. His labors exhibit their ripened fruit but once in a generation. The heedless boy must grow to manhood and the laughing girl become a matron before he can be certain that his labors have not been in vain.

If there are any here whose children are to be educated—fathers—mothers—guardians—let me bespeak of you a feeling of indulgence and sympathy for those to whom the difficult task of instructing them may be confided. They need all your aid in training up your children in the way in which they should go. If you do not find them always patient, remember how often your own patience has been taxed to the utmost, even though strengthened by the warmest sympathies of our nature. If you do not find them always tender, remember that parental tenderness sometimes gives way under strong provocation. If you do not find them faithful, consider how often you yourselves have failed to do all that you might have done for those whom Providence has confided especially to your care.

But, teachers, although your calling may not lead you along the traveled highways of life—though no trump of fame may sound your names abroad—though public applause may not follow you—yet, if you are faithful, you will carry along with you the highest reward and the richest of all consolations—*the consciousness of duty done.* You will see those for whom you have labored—those on whom you have expended the best energies of your bodies and minds, maturing in all that is noble and good. You will see the seeds of intelligence and virtue, planted by your own hands, bring forth their richest fruits. You will sympathise and rejoice in the success of others; and when the evening of life shall come, and you shall look back for the last time on the fading scenes of the past, it will be a pleasing reflection that the day has not been passed in vain, but that you have contributed your full share to that intellectual and moral development which is the glory and renown of a free people, and the only sure foundation of free institutions.

www.ingramcontent.com/pod-product-compliance
Lightning Source LLC
LaVergne TN
LVHW011122110826
845150LV00008B/2227